Pipe Cleaner MANIA

Christine M. Irvin

Children's Press®

A Division of Scholastic Inc.

New York • Toronto • London • Auckland • Sydney

Mexico City • New Delhi • Hong Kong

Danbury, Connecticut

D0813676

The author and publisher are not responsible for injuries or accidents that occur during or from any craft projects. Craft projects should be conducted in the presence of or with the help of an adult. Any instructions of the craft projects that require the use of sharp or other unsafe items should be conducted by or with the help of an adult.

Design and Production by Function Thru Form Inc.
Illustrations by Mia Gomez, Function Thru Form Inc.
Photographs ©: School Tools/Joe Atlas

Library of Congress Cataloging-in-Publication Data

Irvin, Christine M.

      Pipe cleaner mania / by Christine M. Irvin.

        p. cm. — (Craft mania)

      Includes index.

      Summary: Explains how to use common household objects and pipe cleaners to make such things as a daisy, miniature sculptures, a ring toss game, and pencil toppers.

      ISBN 0-516-22279-1 (lib. bdg.)   0-516-27763-4 (pbk.)

      1. Pipe cleaner craft—Juvenile literature. [1. Pipe cleaner craft. 2. Handicraft.] I. Title. II. Series.

TT880 .I793 2002

745.5—dc21

                                  2001008236

CHILDREN'S PRESS and associated logos are trademarks and or registered trademarks of Grolier Publishing Co., Inc.
SCHOLASTIC and associated logos are trademarks and or registered trademarks of Scholastic Inc.

1 2 3 4 5 6 7 8 9 10 R 11 10 09 08 07 06 05 04 03 02

Table of Contents

Welcome to the World of CRAFT MANIA!

Don't throw away that pipe cleaner! Everyday items, such as cardboard tubes and paper plates, can become exciting works of art. You can have fun doing the projects and help save the environment at the same time by recycling these household objects instead of just throwing them away.

You can find ways to reuse many things around your home in craft projects. Bottle caps, buttons, old dried beans, and seeds can become eyes, ears, or a nose for an animal. Instead of buying construction paper, you can use scraps of wrapping paper or even last Sunday's comics to cover your art projects. Save the twist ties from bags of bread or vegetables—they make great legs! These are just a few examples of how you can turn garbage into art. Try to think of other things in your home that can be used in your crafts.

Did You Know?

- Each person creates about 4 pounds (1.8 kilograms) of garbage per day.

- Each person in the United States uses about 580 pounds (260 kg) of paper every year. Businesses in the United States use enough paper to circle the earth 20 times every day!

- Americans use enough cardboard each year to make a paper bale as big as a football field.

- Americans throw away more than 60 billion food and drink cans (like tin cans and soft drink cans) and 28 billion glass bottles and jars (like those from ketchup and pickles) every year.

That's a lot of trash!

What you will need

It's easy to get started on your craft projects. The crafts in this book require some materials you can find around your home, some basic art supplies, and your imagination.

Buttons, bottle caps, beads, old dried beans, or seeds for decoration	**Hole puncher**
Glue	**Construction paper (or newspaper or scraps of wrapping paper)**
Tape	**Felt (or scraps of fabric)**
Tempera paints	
Colored markers	**Twist ties (or pipe cleaners)**

You might want to keep your craft materials in a box so that they will be ready any time you want to start a craft project. Now that you know what you need, look through the book and pick a project to try. Become a Craft Maniac!

A Note to Grown-Ups

Older children will be able to do most of the projects by themselves. Younger ones will need more adult supervision. All of them will enjoy making the items and playing with their finished creations. The directions for most of the crafts in this book require the use of scissors. Do not allow young children to use scissors without adult supervision.

 Helpful Hints

Cutting pipe cleaners can be tricky so make sure to get help from an adult. If a pipe cleaner will not stay twisted together, use a drop of glue to help hold it closed. Tacky glue works better than regular white glue when gluing pipe cleaners.

Wacky Headband

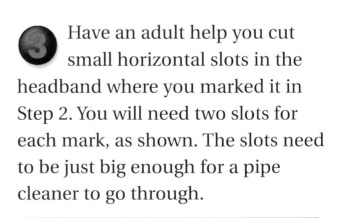

- **Brown paper shopping bag opened to lie flat**
- **Scissors** (Before cutting any material, please ask an adult for help.)
- **Pencil**
- **Two pipe cleaners**
- **Two cotton balls** (or two buttons)
- **Glue**
- **Ruler**

What you do

1 Make the headband. Have an adult help you cut a 2-inch wide strip from the shopping bag big enough to fit around the top of your head, with about ½ inch extra.

2 Use the pencil to mark the headband where you want the antennae attached.

3 Have an adult help you cut small horizontal slots in the headband where you marked it in Step 2. You will need two slots for each mark, as shown. The slots need to be just big enough for a pipe cleaner to go through.

4 Make the antennae. Glue one cotton ball to the end of one pipe cleaner. Do the same with the other cotton ball and pipe cleaner. Let the glue dry before going on to Step 5.

5 Add the antennae. Slide one pipe cleaner end through one of the slots on one side of the headband and out through the other, as shown. Add a drop of glue in the slot to hold the antenna in place. Do the same with the other antenna. Let the glue dry before going on to Step 6.

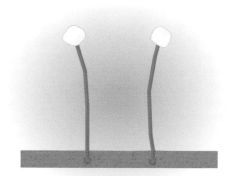

6 Finish your headband. Wrap the headband around your head. Overlap the ends so it fits snugly on your head. Mark with a pencil where you want the headband to end. Take the headband off and put a drop of glue on one side of the headband. Press the two sides of the headband together. Let the glue dry before wearing your headband.

Other Ideas

- Add glitter to the cotton balls to make them sparkle. Put a drop of glue on each cotton ball. Sprinkle glitter onto the glue. When the glue dries, gently tap off the loose glitter.

- Decorate your headband with markers, paints, glitter, or sequins before adding the antennae in Step 5.

- Use pieces of wallpaper for the headband.

Pencil Toppers

What you need

- One large pipe cleaner
- One small pipe cleaner
- Pencil

What you do

1. Make the head of your pencil topper. Bend the large pipe cleaner to make a loop in the middle, as shown. This is your pencil topper's head.

10

2 Make the body and legs. Twist the ends of the pipe cleaner together to make the body. Leave a section of both ends of the pipe cleaner untwisted for the legs.

3 Add the arms. Twist the small pipe cleaner once around the pencil topper's body to make the arms, as shown.

4 Hook your pencil topper to a pencil. Bend one arm and one leg over the sides of a pencil.

Other Ideas

- Give your pencil topper a face. Cut a piece of felt to fit the head section. Glue the felt to the back of the head. Use a felt-tipped marker to draw in eyes, a nose, and a mouth.

- Make multicolored pencil toppers for different occasions. For instance, a red and white one could be used for Valentine's Day. A brown and orange one could be for fall, Halloween, or Thanksgiving. And a green and white one could be used for either spring or St. Patrick's Day.

Bead Bunny

What you need

- Three round beads, each a different size, and each big enough to thread on two pipe cleaners
- Two long pipe cleaners
- Glue
- Marker
- Cotton ball

What you do

1 Make the bunny's body. Thread the beads on both of the pipe cleaners in order from the smallest to the largest, as shown. Leave a larger amount of the pipe cleaners sticking out of the bottom bead for legs. The smallest bead will be the head and the larger beads will be the body.

12

2 Make the ears. Bend the pipe cleaners at the top to make ear shapes, as shown. Put a drop of glue on the top bead to hold the ears in place.

3 Make the feet. Bend the pipe cleaners at the bottom to make feet shapes, as shown. Put a drop of glue on the bottom bead to hold the feet in place.

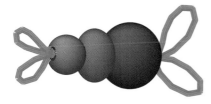

4 Finish your bunny. Use the marker to draw a face on the top bead. Glue a piece of a cotton ball on the back of the bottom bead for a tail. Let the glue dry before playing with your bunny.

Other Ideas

- Glue a bit of cotton on your bunny's face for the nose.

- Glue two tiny beads on your bunny's face for eyes.

- Paint the beads before putting them together in Step 1. Make sure the paint is completely dry before threading the beads onto the pipe cleaners.

- Use different kinds of beads to make an assortment of bunnies.

Silly Glasses

What you need

- **Three pipe cleaners**
- **Scissors** (Before cutting any material, please ask an adult for help.)

What you do

1 Make the lenses section. Fold a pipe cleaner in half. Make a loop using half of the pipe cleaner, as shown. Twist one end of the pipe cleaner around the other to close the first loop. Make another loop with the remaining amount of pipe cleaner. Twist the ends together to close the second loop, as shown.

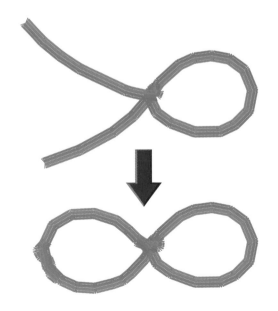

2 Make the sides of the glasses. Bend each of the other two pipe cleaners to make side frames, each with a hook on the end, as shown. The hook part will fit over your ear.

3 Put your glasses together. Twist the straight end of one side piece around one side of the lenses section, as shown. Do the same with the other side piece.

4 Try on your glasses. Bend each side piece to fit around your ears. If there is excess pipe cleaner material, take the glasses off and have an adult help you cut off any excess.

Other Ideas

● Add lenses to your glasses. Wrap the eyeholes with clear or colored plastic wrap.

Flashy Rings

What you need

- Two pipe cleaners, cut in half, for each ring
- One bead or button for each ring
- Scissors (Before cutting any material, please ask an adult for help.)

What you do

 Twist two pipe cleaners around each other, as shown.

2 Make a ring shape. Bend the pipe cleaners around your finger. Do not twist the ends together.

3 Add some decoration. Thread a bead or a button onto the pipe cleaner.

4 Finish your ring. Twist the ends of the pipe cleaner together, as shown. Have an adult help you cut off any excess pipe cleaner material.

That's it! Your ring is ready to wear.

Other Ideas

- Make an assortment of rings using different colors of pipe cleaners and different beads and buttons.

- Make bracelets instead of rings. You will need one pipe cleaner, uncut, for each bracelet. Bend the pipe cleaner into a circle shape, big enough to fit around your wrist, with a little left over. Add beads or buttons to the pipe cleaner for decorations. Bend both ends of the pipe cleaner to make hooks. Slide the bracelet onto your wrist and hook the ends together.

Pretty Daisy

What you need

- **Two long white pipe cleaners**
- **One yellow pipe cleaner**
- **One long green pipe cleaner**
- **Scissors (Before cutting any materials, please ask an adult for help.)**

What you do

1 Make the center of your daisy. Have an adult help you cut the yellow pipe cleaner in half. Bend one half of the yellow pipe cleaner into a circle. Twist the ends together to close the circle, as shown.

2 Add the petals. Twist one end of one of the white pipe cleaners around the yellow pipe cleaner circle. Bend the white pipe cleaner into a small loop. Wrap it around the circle, as shown, to make the first petal. Continue adding petals until

18

you reach the end of the white pipe cleaner. End with a full loop petal. Wrap the second white pipe cleaner around the circle and continue making petals until you have petals all around the circle.

3 Make a stem and leaves. Bend the green pipe cleaner stem to make two leaves, as shown. Make a loop where you want a leaf on the stem. Then wrap the pipe cleaner around the base of the loop. Make a second loop where you want your second leaf. Wrap the pipe cleaner around the base of the second loop.

4 Attach the daisy's head section to the stem section. Twist the top of the stem pipe cleaner once or twice around the edge of the yellow pipe cleaner to hold it in place.

Other Ideas

- Make Brown-Eyed Susans. Use a short brown pipe cleaner for the center of the flower and long orange pipe cleaners for the petals.

- Make your daisy into a refrigerator magnet. Skip Steps 3 and 4. Instead, have an adult help you cut a piece of a white paper bag to fit the flower center. Glue the paper in place on the back of the flower's center. Then glue a magnet to the back of the paper. Let the glue dry before you stick your flower head magnet to the refrigerator.

- Make a daisy hair barrette. Skip Steps 3 and 4. Instead, have an adult help you cut a piece of a white paper bag to fit the flower center. Glue the paper in place on the back of the flower's center. Glue the daisy head to a hair barrette. Let the glue dry before wearing your barrette.

Ring Toss Game

What you need

- One pipe cleaner for each ring
- Several plastic bottles (such as empty soda bottles) to use as targets
- Small pebbles, seeds, or beans

What you do

1 Make rings. Bend each pipe cleaner to make a circle. Twist the ends of the pipe cleaner to hold the circle together, as shown.

Add small pebbles, seeds, or beans to the bottles to weigh them down.

 Set up several bottles on the floor.

That's it! Now you're ready to play the Ring Toss Game. Stand back a few steps from the bottles. Throw a ring and try to make it fall over the neck of a bottle. Score one point for each ring you get on one of the bottles.

Other Ideas

- Make different sizes of rings using different sizes of pipe cleaners.

- Experiment with different sizes of rings and bottles. Is it easier to ring a small-necked bottle with a small ring or a large one? What about a bottle with a big neck?

Buzzy the Bumblebee

What you need

- Three black pipe cleaners
- One yellow pipe cleaner
- One bead, for the head, big enough to thread on a pipe cleaner
- Glue
- Pencil
- Marker

What you do

1 Give your bumblebee a head. Thread one end of a black pipe cleaner through the bead. Bend the end of the pipe cleaner over so it will not fit back through the hole in the bead. Put a drop of glue on the end of the pipe cleaner to hold the bead in place.

2 Make the wings. Using a black pipe cleaner, bring both ends to the center of the pipe cleaner, making a loop. Twist one end around the center of the pipe cleaner and then twist the other end around the center.

3 Add the wings. Place the pipe cleaner with the bead between the two loops of the other black pipe cleaner. Wrap one of the loops around the pipe cleaner with the bead to secure the wings, as shown.

4 Make the body. Twist the last black pipe cleaner and the yellow pipe cleaner together to make one thick, two-colored pipe cleaner. Then, wrap the two-colored pipe cleaner around the pencil, as shown. Slide the pipe cleaners off the pencil.

5 Put your bumblebee together. Thread the end of the beaded pipe cleaner through the twisted two-colored pipe cleaners, as shown. Bend the single black pipe cleaner back slightly to connect the body and head sections.

6 Add the face. Draw in eyes and a mouth with the marker.

Other Ideas

- Use tiny beads for the eyes.
- For wider bumblebee body, try wrapping the yellow and black pipe cleaners around a handful of pencils or a thick marker.
- Make your bumblebee into a lapel pin. Glue a large safety pin to the back of your bumblebee. Let the glue dry before wearing your bumblebee lapel pin.
- Make your bumblebee into a magnet. Glue a magnet to the back of your bumblebee. Let the glue dry. Stick your bumblebee magnet to the refrigerator.

Fun Mini-Sculptures

What you need

- Two large pipe cleaners for each sculpture
- One large, flat button with two holes
- One small cotton ball or a piece of cotton
- Glue
- Two small beads (for eyes)
- Fabric scraps
- Scissors (Before cutting any material, please ask an adult for help.)
- One bottle cap

What you do

1 Make the head and arms of your sculpture. Bend a pipe cleaner in the middle to make a loop for the head. Twist part of the pipe cleaner together to make the neck. Then, bend both ends of the pipe cleaner to make arms, as shown.

2 Add legs to your sculpture. Thread one end of the other pipe cleaner up through one hole in the button and then down through the other hole. Hook both ends of the pipe cleaner legs to the head and arms section. Then, twist the top of the leg section together to hold the arms in place and make the body, as shown.

3 Add a face. Glue a cotton ball to the front of the head section of your sculpture. Then, glue the beads in place on the cotton for eyes.

4 Finish your sculpture. Using the scissors, have an adult help you cut clothes shapes from the fabric scraps, as shown. Glue the clothes in place on your sculpture.

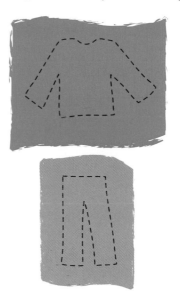

5 Make a stand. Glue the button to the inside of the bottle cap. Let the glue dry before playing with your sculpture.

Other Ideas

- Make your sculptures multicultural by dressing them in ethnic outfits. Try making Japanese kimonos, Mexican serapes, or Indian saris.

- Try making animals instead of people. See if you can make a tiger, a bear, or a flamingo.

Little Mouse

What you need

- **One pipe cleaner**
- **Pencil**
- **Piece of newspaper** (for the ears)
- **Scissors** (Before cutting any material, please ask an adult for help.)

- **Glue**
- **Cotton ball** (for the head)
- **Three tiny seeds** (for eyes and nose)
- **Two small pieces of thread** (for whiskers)

What you do

1 Make the body. Twist the pipe cleaner around the pencil, as shown. Leave about 2 inches of the pipe cleaner straight. Slide the pipe cleaner off the pencil.

2 Add the head. Glue the cotton ball head to the end of the body section, as shown. Let the glue dry before going on to Step 3.

3 Add the ears. Have an adult help you cut two small ear shapes from the newspaper, as shown. Glue the ear shapes to the head.

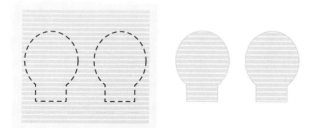

5 Add the face. Glue two seeds in place on the mouse's head for the eyes. Glue the two pieces of thread in place on the head for the whiskers. Glue the last seed in the middle of the whiskers for the nose. Let the glue dry before playing with your mouse.

4 Make the tail. Bend the end of the pipe cleaner to make it curved, as shown.

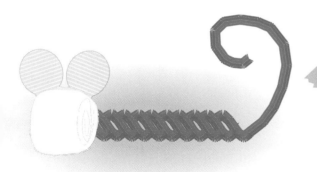

Other Ideas

- Make your mouse into a lapel pin. Glue a large safety pin to one side of your mouse's body. Let the glue dry before wearing your lapel pin.

- Make your mouse into a refrigerator magnet. Glue a magnet to one side of your mouse's body. Let the glue dry before sticking your mouse to the refrigerator or other magnetic surface.

Walking Stick Insect

What you need

- **Four long pipe cleaners**
- **One small bead** (for the head)
- **Scissors** (Before cutting any material, please ask an adult for help.)
- **Marker**

What you do

1 Make the body. Thread the bead onto the end of one of the pipe cleaners. Bend the end of the pipe cleaner back against the bead just enough to keep the bead from sliding off the pipe cleaner.

2 Make the legs. Have an adult help you cut two pipe cleaners in half. Three pieces will be used for legs. One piece will be used for the antennae.

3 Add the antennae. Take one piece of pipe cleaner and put it under the pipe cleaner body just behind the bead. Make sure that there is an even amount of the pipe cleaner on each side. Then wrap the pipe cleaner piece around the body, as shown.

4 Shape the legs. Take one half of a pipe cleaner and make it into a V shape. Then bend each end of the pipe cleaner into a small circle, as shown. You can use your fingers to mold the circles.

5 Add the legs. Put the first set of legs slightly behind the antennae. Add the pipe cleaner with the point up over the pipe cleaner body. Wrap the pipe cleaner around the body. Add the second set of legs about halfway from the end of the body and wrap the pipe cleaner legs around the body. Add the last set of legs at the end of the body and wrap it around the body, as shown.

6 Add the last pipe cleaner. Twist one end of the pipe cleaner in front of the first set of legs. Then wrap the other end of pipe cleaner around the end of the body. Have an adult help you cut off any excess pipe cleaner.

7 Add a face. Use the marker to make eyes and a mouth on the bead.

Other Ideas

- Make a spider. Make four legs instead of three, and make them all the same size. Skip Step 3. Twist the legs in place on the spider's body without leaving any spaces between them. After you put on the last leg, have an adult help you cut off the end of the body pipe cleaner so it is only about ½ inch long. Bend the end of the pipe cleaner back over the last leg.

- Make a scorpion. Make four legs instead of three, and make them all the same size. Add pincers in Step 3 instead of antennae.

29

Family Tree

What you need

- One stick for the tree trunk
- Pipe cleaners for the branches
- Lump of modeling clay
- Lid from a large spray can
- Construction paper

- Scissors (Before cutting any material, please ask an adult for help.)
- Twist ties
- Hole puncher

What you do

1. Make a tree. Twist pipe cleaners around the stick to make branches, as shown. Make three sets of branches.

2 Put your tree in a pot. Fill the spray can lid with modeling clay. Push the end of the stick all the way down into the clay.

3 Make the leaves. Have an adult help you cut leaf shapes from the colored paper, as shown. You will need one leaf for each member of your family—yourself, your parents, your brothers and sisters, and your grandparents. Write the name of a family member on each leaf.

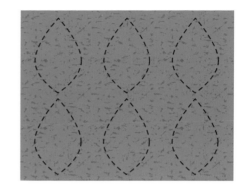

4 Add the leaves. Make a hole in one leaf with the hole puncher. Thread a twist tie through the hole. Wrap the twist tie around one of the branches, as shown. Repeat this process with each of the remaining leaves. Place your grandparents on the upper branches, your parents on the middle branches, and you and your brothers and sisters on the lower ones.

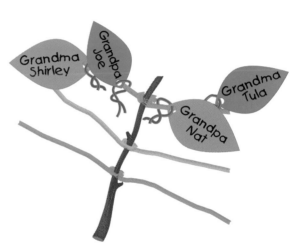

Other Ideas

- Glue small photos of family members to the branches instead of making paper or felt leaves. Have an adult help you cut the photos into leaf shapes, if you like.

- Add smaller branches to your tree by wrapping short pieces of pipe cleaner around the long pipe cleaner branches.

Index

About the Author

Christine M. Irvin lives in the Columbus, Ohio area with her husband, her three children, and her dog. She enjoys writing, reading, doing arts and crafts, and shopping.